Mother Nature Explains:

Polarity and Our Struggle with the Other Side

Mother Nature Notes: Volume 1

Mother Nature explains:
polarity and our struggle
with the other
side

misna burelli

Acknowledgments

Thank you,
Mother Nature,
for Sharing Your
Secrets with us

CONTENTS

Wisdom from Mother Nature: A Recipe for Coming Together

Introduction

If you have been following us through our adventures in "Polarized", you already know that Mother Nature—the ultimate wisdom bearer—has solutions to every problem. In this new series we will reiterate and expand some of the themes covered in "Polarized", while explaining each major concept in smaller, less daunting "Notes".

We will start the series by asking Mother Nature a few questions about one of the most pressing and fundamental issues of our time: polarity. Covered by Carl Jung and more recently by Jordan Peterson, polarity is both a philosophical concept and a natural phenomenon.

We would like to thank Mother Nature for taking the time to explain this difficult concept, and we would like to invite you along for the ride, paving the way for the exploration of related yet distant ideas which will be covered in future volumes.

As always, we welcome your feedback.

Visit us at: ImmuneAdvantageSolution.com
or email us at: **info@immuneadvantagesolution.com**

We are looking forward to your comments!

MOTHER NATURE EXPLAINS: POLARITY

What Carl Jung has got to do with it

One of the most famous quotes attributed to Carl Jung is, "No tree... can grow to heaven unless its roots reach down to hell".[1] Many of us intuitively understand the essence of the quote, acknowledging its truth. Jungian analyst Jordan Peterson also values this quote because it is profound, touching one of life's greatest mysteries: polarity.[2]

---

[1] Carl Jung and the C.G. Jung Foundation for Analytical Psychology www.cgjungny.org
[2] Jordan B. Peterson *12 Rules for Life: An Antidote to Chaos*, Random House Canada, **2018,** page 180

Polarity has been a recurring concept throughout history and many disciplines. From Taoism to great psychoanalysts such as Jung, societies and individuals have theorized about it. We all know about the ying and yang or the dark side versus the light as an often-observed element of polarity.

But what is polarity? One could reduce it to a simple plus versus minus on a scale where the middle is neutral. Or alternatively, a yes or no to a clear-cut question. But usually it is more complicated than that. Perhaps we should say polarity is something that expresses itself on opposite ends of a spectrum, where the root cause or the fundamental basic origin is the same.

Allow me to expand on that thought to include a simple example from everyday life: when not feeling well, many of us (not everyone) are either really thirsty or completely thirstless, but not in between. In the middle, between the two poles, we would be feeling just right—not too thirsty and not too thirstless. That is the state we are aiming for when recovery has taken place.

The above is an example of polarity displayed on the body's physical level, but we can notice such things happening on other levels as well including our mental/emotional makeup. Let's see how that could feel. Suppose a person named Jack is very healthy. Looking at him, one can observe mostly positive personality or character traits. But as his health weakens, he loses these positive attributes, and what was originally a strength, will now become a liability. It could appear like this:

Jack is detail oriented and works in an environment with numbers—a tax office. He is happy, as he has a natural ability to check and double check records; he is extremely reliable, consistently ensuring that things are 150% correct. His job is perfect for him because the environment fits his personality, and he is satisfied and successful.

But now imagine him sick. Where is he most vulnerable? There are two possibilities: he could become tired, losing concentration, performing poorly, mixing up numbers and forgetting what he wanted to do. Losing his edge. Letting his job become a monotonous drudgery at an uninspiring 50% effort. Or, on the flip side, he could over-do what he's good at. He could perform at 300% instead of 150%. So, you say that's even better? At first glance, it may appear advantageous. However, at that level of meticulousness, he's bogging down and stressing out over every new client, going home too late, and letting things move too slowly; he's too stubborn and never satisfied with the result. Others will inevitably start avoiding him because he's too detail oriented, becoming a difficult person to work with. They will notice that things get stuck in his office. Ultimately, his reputation will suffer. His greatest strength will become his greatest weakness as his health deteriorates.

Polarity is a Principle

This is just one example, but there are countless others because polarity is a principle. Polarities are the extreme tendencies we have when we are unwell. When balanced and healthy they are mostly invisible—not too much and not too little of the peculiarities, strengths and weaknesses that make up our character. But when times are bad—when we are off balance—even former strengths can become real liabilities, and former liabilities are not useful, without the context of the positive pole.

Another common case of polarities extending too far to one side often happens around compassion. Even though the healthy range of emotions can reach pretty far on both sides, there have recently been some very clear cases of people going overboard with their feelings in one direction only. In their overly positive state, these formerly great warriors for truth, justice, and equality, have now shifted their goal to help the unfortunate into a kind of self-abandoning tournament. In their attempt to stand out and save the world, their priorities get mixed up, and they cannot distinguish between worthy goals, realistic goals, and self-destructive goals. Their objective is now only compassion, no matter the price.

Anxiety and depression follow the same patterns. The target is not to aim for an anxiety level of zero on the far side of the positive pole. Anxiety is a useful warning signal that keeps you out of trouble when confronted with uncertainty and danger. But too much anxiety makes life miserable. It's like living with the alarm permanently set on emergency. And that would be life on the edge of the negative pole.

The same is true for depression. On the positive end of the pole we can't and shouldn't demand to only have blissfully happy days. To never feel unhappy would make us into robots. We should mourn our losses and feel our pains just like humans do, but we should not get so overwhelmed that we can't cope; we should not behave like someone just died every day, which is the end of the negative pole. The state with both emotions present is the most appropriate.

MOTHER NATURE EXPLAINS: POLARITY

Missing the Forest for the Trees

Let's go back to Jung's "tree quote" (no tree... can grow to heaven unless its roots reach down to hell) and see how it applies to this. The quote represents the ideal balanced archetype with strong characteristics covering both positive and negative poles. The unbalanced positive archetype would be too much of a good thing. With the negative pole missing, this could be a person that's way too innocent, nice, and trusting, eventually becoming a victim of bullying. The outcome will be self-destruction or enslavement, simply because there is no self-preservation. The unbalanced negative archetype would be this: not enough of a good thing which could lead all the way from being too difficult, suspicious, mean, aggressive, violent, without a conscience, to outright evil. Since there is nothing good left in this case, it's more obvious that it will lead straight to disaster.

Being on both pole ends is problematic, while the middle, which contains parts of both poles, is the ideal and strongest archetype. If you cannot identify the middle, where self-protection and compassion are both adequately present, you are vulnerable to both extremes, because as soon as you realize that one pole gave you dangerous exposure to being abused, you switch over to the other side, which is full of revenge and bitterness. The rage that can set in here puts you straight on the far negative end of the spectrum—into the "hell" area.

Sometimes I see commentary that's missing the point. People who say, "what nonsense, Jung's quote is encouraging me to be evil!". This is a complete misinterpretation and shows a lack of understanding reality as it is. It is not he, who has the *most evil* within, is also the strongest, nor he who is strongest must be evil. Instead, it is he who has both *some* evil and good parts *balanced together*, in the right way, will be strongest. It's the balance that counts!

The danger that pole extremes switch sides can happen in many ways. For example, when a workaholic is suddenly too exhausted to work, or violent revolutionaries give up and withdraw in frustration, they will internalize their feelings in an unhealthy, self-destructive way. Or again, when a bully becomes a coward, after being confronted by an even bigger bully. For individuals, societies, and the world as a whole, it is a good idea to stay in the middle. Weak, imbalanced archetypes, at the pole extremes, are much more dangerous than strong, balanced ones, even though the middle always contains parts of both extremes.

Polarities give people a chance to foresee how they might be vulnerable, allowing them to take active steps to prevent sliding onto the pole extremes. If I know, for example, that I tend to be a workaholic, I might be very careful to watch myself. Maybe my work attitude has served me well in terms of career and success, but I can tell that sometimes I have the tendency to go overboard with it. This tendency of "too much of a good thing" might wreck my health and push me off balance. Therefore, I might be on the lookout for burnout, the other side of the spectrum. I might make it a point to accept related criticism from my husband or wife without reacting angrily. I might also try to analyze the situation and find out why I'm off balance—be it a stressful work situation or a health problem.

MOTHER NATURE EXPLAINS: POLARITY

Our Struggle

It is true that we, as humans, have trouble coping with the concept of polarity. It makes us uneasy to find both poles within us, and some of us think that seeing the "shadow"—as Jung calls the other side—is pathological and should be avoided at all cost. It can feel good, out there on the pole ends, because without doubting that we are doing the right thing, we feel morally superior. Ignorance is bliss. But that is not what we want. We want to incorporate the shadow in a productive and balanced manner. We should be strong enough to deal with the shadow. We should work on it. Similarly, if we understand Peterson's concept of consciousness and meaning as the middle between order and chaos, we recognize that he is saying the same thing. His recommendation to "position yourself where the terror of existence is under control and you are secure, but where you are also alert and engaged" is meant as advice to place yourself between the positive and negative pole—into the productive and life affirming section of the spectrum. He is making a case *against* extreme polarity and *for* balance.[3]

To sum it up: Polarity is a universal principle that is visible everywhere in our society (or in the universe?) that affects everyone—including you! It is obvious that we, as a society, have become more unbalanced recently. Many people have become so polarized that they can't even talk to others from the opposing camp. That is what it means to be polarized: to not have even a little bit of the other side inside you and to not understand the other side at all. It is clearly a dangerous path we are on. An imbalanced path. Just like the archetype who needs both opposing poles, our society needs to be able to accommodate these opposite viewpoints without hate, blame and major unrest. If we are not able to do that peacefully and find our true

---

[3] Jordan B. Peterson *12 Rules for Life: An Antidote to Chaos*, Random House Canada, **2018,** pages 35-44

middle, extreme polarity will take us over the edge and it doesn't even matter which side of the cliff we fall off because usually the two opposing ends are connected more than we would like to admit and can easily morph into each other. They are two sides of the same coin.

MOTHER NATURE EXPLAINS: POLARITY

A New Direction

Where do we go from here? My hope for the future is that we recognize polarity as the problem it is. We can all make a commitment to try and recognize it in ourselves. We can all make an effort to minimize it. When we recognize it in others, we don't need to indulge it. Instead, we can ask them why they feel so strongly about a particular topic. If they are willing, we can gently steer them towards exploring the other side, so that, over time, we will all land more or less in the middle. That would bring benefits to us all.[4]

---

[4] Misna Burelli and Lena Kratz *Polarized: Carl Jung, Jordan Peterson, Samuel Hahnemann, Greta Thunberg, and the Devouring Mother are going to a party,* **2019**

Index